THIS WALKER BOOK BELONGS TO:

_____

_____

_____

THE SHAPE-CHANGER

"There is a great spell on this valley and bad things happen to anyone who comes here."

When young Kari, the son of Viking settlers, rides in to a neighbouring valley one day, he meets the most striking girl he has ever seen. Her name is Ellen, the daughter of Colman, and she tells Kari of the terrible spell that has been put on their homestead. Kari is determined to help break the spell, but he soon discovers the full force of the strange and frightening magic he is up against – the cruel magic of the shape-changer. How will he, a mere boy, be able to overcome such trickery?

WALKER STORYBOOKS

Staples for Amos by Alison Morgan
The Shape-Changer by Julian Atterton
Robin Hood and the Miller's Son
    by Julian Atterton
Robin Hood and Little John by Julian Atterton
Earthquake by Ruskin Bond
We Three Kings of Pepper Street Prime
    by Joan Smith

^{The} Shape-Changer

First published 1985 by
Julia MacRae Books
This edition published 1989 by
Walker Books Ltd, 87 Vauxhall Walk,
London SE11 5HJ

Text © 1985 Julian Atterton
Illustrations © 1985 Nigel Murray

Printed in Great Britain by
Richard Clay Ltd, Bungay, Suffolk

British Library Cataloguing in Publication Data
Atterton, Julian
The shape-changer.
I. Title   II. Murray, Nigel
823'.914[J]   PZ7
ISBN 0-7445-1385-5

The Shape-Changer

Written by
JULIAN ATTERTON

Illustrated by
NIGEL MURRAY

WALKER BOOKS
LONDON

Contents

1 The Settlers, 7

2 The Spell, 15

3 The Wise Woman, 23

4 The Broken Man, 32

5 Kari's Run, 41

6 Magic at Sunrise, 52

1 The Settlers

One morning a thousand years ago, late in spring, a tall Viking and his wife and son could be seen riding up Eskdale in the moors of northern England.

They rode until they came to where the valley forked into two smaller dales made by streams that came twisting down out of the High Moor. There the tall Viking stopped his horse and turned to his wife.

"Tell me, Halla," he asked her, "is this the place you saw in your dream?"

"Yes," she said. "This is the place we crossed the sea to find."

"Well, it looks good to me," said the Viking, whose name was Olaf. "The forests will need clearing, but we will never go short of timber, and we can intake the moors to make sheep pasture. I say we make our home in the wider of the two dales. All we need now is a name for it."

"I should name it Westerdale," said their boy, whose own name was Kari, "because the lie of it means that the sun will always set over the dale head."

So they named it Westerdale, and there they built their farmstead. Things went hard at first, but after a few years had gone by they were prospering. Olaf was bringing in rich harvests and had a fine flock of sheep, and Halla had given birth to three more children. The farmers of Eskdale spoke of them as good neighbours who were always generous with their help or advice.

Kari by this time was growing up, and all who knew him considered him an even-tempered and reliable lad who was always ready to do anyone a good turn. Every spring he made it his custom to take the sheep up to a shieling he had built in a narrow valley that

curled away into the moors on the northern side
of Westerdale. There he lived alone with them
during the long months of the summer grazing.

One year, just before the barley harvest,
there was a powerful storm which thundered
and flashed over the moors for a day and a
night. The rain came down so hard that all Kari
could do was huddle in his shieling and try to
keep his fire alight, and when he came out in
the morning, he found that the sheep had
broken out of their fold and run away in terror.
At first he thought nothing of it, and spent the
morning drying his clothes, but when at
midday the sky was clear blue and the sheep
had not returned, he began to get worried.

He bridled his pony and followed the sheep-
tracks up onto the open moor, and after a while

he found the sheep grazing happily in a hollow in the heather. It was only after he had herded them back to the shieling and counted them into the sheepfold that he realised that five were still missing. He gave the skies a dirty look and turned his pony round to start the search all over again.

He was still searching when the day drew in and the light began to wane. As a last effort, he decided to ride over to the rim of the second of the valleys that forked away from the head of Eskdale. He had never been there before, and all he knew was that it was farmed by an Irishman named Colman who had not been living there long.

From the rim of Colman's Dale, he found himself looking down into a valley much like his father's. It was a swathe of treetops broken only by the marsh meadows and a farmstead clearing surrounded by fields of golden barley ready for harvest, and in the soft light of the evening it looked a peaceful place. The valley slopes were gentle except for just above the farmstead where a crag jutted out of the moor,

and it was as he took this in that Kari caught
sight of his five missing sheep lying on their
backs at the foot of the rocks.

He galloped down to them but they were all
as dead as they looked. It was the first time he
had ever lost any of his flock, and it hurt him
so much that he dropped to the ground and
wailed with grief. He had not been there long
before he heard footsteps cracking twigs in the
woods below and turned to see a girl walking
towards him from the farmstead. Her eyes were
as green as oak leaves at midsummer, and her

11

hair was as brown as bracken in autumn and fell to her waist in a cascade of tangled tresses. Beneath her cloak she wore a dress of brocaded silk that was much too large for her and had certainly seen better days, but the strange effect of this did nothing to stop Kari from thinking her the most striking girl he had ever seen.

"Greeting to you, Stranger," she said.
"These sheep were here when the sun rose this
morning. Are they yours?"

Kari said they were and asked the girl her
name.

"I am Ellen, the daughter of Colman," she
replied. "Now tell me who you are."

Kari told her his name and looked again at
his sheep. "This is more than bad luck," he
said sadly, "that they should run into the valley
at the one place where there is a crag to fall
over."

"Much more than bad luck," said Ellen.
"There is a great spell on this valley and bad
things happen to anyone who comes here."

Kari looked into her eyes and saw she meant
what she said, then he looked up at the fast
darkening sky. "That's as may be," he said,
"but it is too late for me to ride home and I
would be grateful if you could give me shelter
here tonight."

"That I can only do if you give me a
promise," said Ellen.

He asked her what it was.

13

"You must promise not to take it as an insult if my father gives you no welcome," she replied.

"That seems little enough to ask," said Kari. "You have my word on it."

The girl nodded almost unhappily and turned away into the woods. Kari had a sudden feeling that night on the open moor might be better than the strangeness he was about to walk into, but he shrugged it off, took his pony by the reins and followed Ellen down towards the farmstead.

2   The Spell

He soon saw the reason for the promise the girl
had asked of him.

Colman the Irishman sat stone-faced and
silent in the hall of the farmhouse. He did not
even look up when Kari and Ellen entered, but
sat staring into the fire with a horn of beer
clasped in one hand. Kari could tell that he had
once been a tall and fine-looking man, but now
his face sagged and his shoulders slumped and
there seemed no spirit left in him.

There was one other man in the place, a
Norseman named Grim whose left leg was so
lame that Kari guessed no other farmer would
hire him. Grim ate the food that Ellen set in
front of him, then wandered off to his sleeping-

place, leaving Kari with the feeling that he was in for a dismal evening.

The food was no better than the company.

The bread had no taste, the cheese had less flavour than a handful of snow, and the barley beer was no better than brackish water with soil stirred into it.

"You asked me not to take your father's lack of welcome as an insult," he said to Ellen, "so I hope you will not be insulted by the question

16

I want to ask. Why is it that you eat so miserably when you live on such a rich farmstead?"

Ellen blushed. "I told you," she said, "there is a great spell on this valley."

"And yet," said Kari, "when I looked down from the rim of the moor I saw fine fields of barley and a herd of dairy cattle. If I had such a farm I could make beer and cheese that would be the envy of Eskdale."

"Not here," said Ellen. "For years now the barley has been destroyed on the night before the harvest, and the milk vanishes from the cows' udders so they have nothing to yield in the morning."

"The barley looks ripe to me now," he said. "If you like I can help you bring it in."

"Before you came, we were talking of harvesting tomorrow," she replied, "but we know it will not come to that. That is why tonight my father is even more silent than usual."

"It seems to me," said Kari, "that if things are so bad, you should pack up and move on.

There is good land for the clearing over in Westerdale, and my father has a name for helping his neighbours."

Ellen shook her head. "My father says he has no hope of moving on, and that the spell will follow him wherever he goes. I would give anything to be away, but I cannot leave him here alone."

Kari looked into her eyes, and the sorrow in them moved him more than anything had moved him in all his life.

"Ellen," he said, "I give you my word that I will not rest until I have broken the spell that hangs over this valley."

"Do not make rash promises you cannot keep," she warned.

Kari could think of no reply, but he wrapped his cloak around him and went out into the night. The fields of barley were rippling gently in the moonlight, and the cows were grazing contentedly in the garth. He decided to sit down on a rock and wait to see what happened, and he passed the time by thinking of Ellen.

The night went by, and he had almost fallen

into a doze when something made him shiver
and the hairs prickled on the back of his neck.
He turned to see a huge black wolf slinking out
of the woods. It was as large as a pony, and in
no time at all it had gone from cow to cow and
sucked the milk from their udders while they
stood as if rooted to the ground. Then it loped
past Kari, giving him a long look with two
baleful yellow eyes, and bounded into the
fields of barley and leapt about chewing the
heads off the stalks until in no time at all there
was nothing left but a trampled mass of stubble.

When that was done the wolf padded back
past Kari, licking its lips and yawning, and
made off the way it had come.

"Well," said Kari to himself in a shaken voice, "there is a strange beast if ever there was one, but all beasts can be hunted, and the best thing I can do now is track it back to its lair so I know where it lives."

He hurried into the wood and soon caught sight of the wolf, which took one look at him and broke into a run. It bounded effortlessly up onto the moor, across which it set off so fast that Kari had to run his hardest just to keep it in sight. Luckily the moon was full and the sky clear, for if the night had been cloudy the black wolf would soon have been invisible against the dark mass of the heather; and luckily the wolf had a stomach full of milk and barley to slow it down, so that by and by Kari began to close the gap between them.

The wolf plunged down into a wild valley that wound north into the moors out of Colman's Dale, and it was there that Kari drew level with it.

"Now, my greedy friend," he said breathlessly, "you know I can keep up with you, so let's see where you want to run to."

The wolf's answer was to turn on Kari, bare its fangs and spring at him. Kari threw up his arms to protect his face and throat, but all he felt against them was a flapping of wings, and as he fell back into the heather he saw a large

white swan beating up into the sky. He jumped back onto his feet but the wolf was nowhere to be seen. There was only the swan high above him, slowly flying off into the night.

"This is beyond me," he whispered to the empty moor, and he turned and set off back towards Colman's Dale.

21

It was daylight when he reached the farmstead, where Colman, Grim and Ellen were standing looking at the wreckage of the barley. Ellen ran to meet him.

"We thought the spell had carried you off," she said, then her voice tailed away. There was a look in Kari's eyes that made her take a step backwards.

He told them what had happened.

"No surprise to me that," said Colman. "This is a curse that can take any shape." He stumbled off towards the farmhouse like a blind man. Grim wiped his nose with his sleeve and limped away.

"You see," said Ellen gently, "you cannot help us."

"I must go and ask my father what to do about this," said Kari, "then I will return."

"You will never return," said Ellen. "Your father will tell you to go back to your sheep and leave us to our fate."

Kari knew she was right but he could not bring himself to admit it. He took his pony and rode back over the moor towards Westerdale.

22

3   The Wise Woman

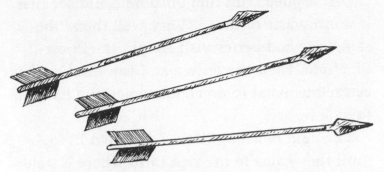

Olaf was harvesting his barley when he saw his
son riding down off the moor. He greeted him
with open arms and Kari told him about the
five sheep.

"That's too bad," said Olaf, "but these things
happen."

Then Kari told him about the spell that hung
over Colman's Dale and of how he had chased
the black wolf.

"Now you really do worry me," said Olaf.
"If you go round getting entangled in other
people's bad luck you can hardly expect to
wear out many more new shirts."

"That's as may be," said Kari, "but I gave
my word I would break the spell, and I intend

to keep it."

Olaf argued with him until he could see that it was a waste of time. "Very well then," he said, "we had better visit Harald the Priest-Chieftain. He is the only man I can think of who can tell us what to do about something like this."

The next morning they rode down Eskdale until they came to the rich farm where Harald lived. He gave them a warm welcome and asked them the reason for their journey.

"We have come to ask for your advice," said Olaf.

"You certainly deserve any advice I can give you," replied Harald, pouring them some ale.

Then Kari told his story while Harald listened and stroked his beard, which was one of the longest in Eskdale.

"That's a weird story," said Harald, "and the meaning of it is quite beyond me. These Irish are not your kin and the best advice I can give you is to leave them to their fate and keep an eye on your sheep."

"I'm sure your words are full of wisdom," said Kari, "but I gave my word I would break the spell, and I intend to keep it."

"Big words for one so small," said Harald, stroking his beard harder than ever. "Perhaps you had better visit Hild the Deep-Minded who lives over at Horn End in Farndale. She is the only person in these parts who can tell you what to do about something like this."

Olaf and Kari thanked him and rode away.

"Which is the way to Farndale?" asked Kari.

"I had a feeling you were going to ask me that," said his father. "It's a day's ride to the west over the High Moor. This would have to happen in the middle of the barley harvest."

"You see to the harvest," said Kari, "and
I'll see to my fate."

Early the next morning he set off, and all day
he rode over the High Moor, past the standing
stones and burial mounds which were the only
signs that people had ever been there. Late in

the afternoon the rolling heather seemed to
open beneath his feet and he found himself
looking down on the woods and farmsteads of
Farndale.

Hild the Deep-Minded lived at Horn End with her three sons, and she watched Kari ride up with eyes that were misty blue like clouds over the sea. She gave him a good welcome and asked him the reason for his journey.

"I need to know how to break a spell," he said, "and I've been told you're the only person in these parts who can give me advice on that."

"The first thing to understand," said Hild, "is that spells are only ever cast for a very strong reason, and an outsider needs a very strong reason of his own if he wants to break one. How do I know that you deserve any advice I can give you?"

"You have a name for being wise," said Kari with a smile, "so I'm sure you can think of a way to find out."

"Very well," said Hild, and she led him out

to a field on the valley slope. "Build me a sheepfold in three days and three nights, and I'll tell you at the end of it if you deserve my advice."

Kari set to work at once, and spent the whole night and the next day collecting stone from the broken crags on the edge of the moor. Hild sent her sons to him with food and drink, but she had forbidden them to help, and it was well into the second day before he had even laid the

foundations of the sheepfold. As the moon rose on his third night in Farndale, he was bruised in every limb and moving like a sleepwalker, and there were moments when he dropped to the ground and lay there thinking he would never rise again; but each time he remembered the sorrow in Ellen's green eyes and somehow found the strength to drag himself to his feet and go back to his work.

Just before sunset on the third day he laid the last stones in place and turned to see Hild walking towards him.

"Now do you think I deserve your advice?" he asked her.

"I see you can do the task," she said, "but I still have to see how well you have done it."

She walked around the outside of the sheepfold, leaning against the walls to test them, then walked through the gateway and did the same inside. When she came out she was smiling.

"This is well done," she said. "You could have worked only during the days and built walls of a single thickness which would fall down in a winter or two, but instead you worked day and night and built a double wall which will still be here when your children are my age. That is enough to tell me you are someone who does things well and for good reasons, and that you deserve all the advice I can give you."

Kari told her all about the spell that hung over Colman's Dale.

"It seems to me," said Hild, "that you are up against a Shape-Changer, a creature who can change its shape at will and has some grudge against Colman. I can tell you how to track it down, but breaking the spell will be a harder thing altogether."

"First things first," said Kari. "How do I track it down?"

"You must make three arrows from the wood of a rowan tree you have never seen before,

then you must lie in wait for the Shape-Changer and hit it in the ankle with one of them. Once it has been struck it will be unable to change its shape and will make a run for its lair. You must give chase and be with it at sunrise, for that is when it will change back into the shape it began life in, and once you have seen it in its true form you will have power over it."

"Will I have the power to break the spell?" asked Kari.

"That I cannot tell you," she replied. "The Shape-Changer may not in itself be the spell, but only part of it . . . but if ever you get as far as that you will be able to see a good way further than you or I can now. Every spell has a root which needs to be dug up and burnt. I suggest you find out all you can about Colman and why he thinks he is a person who deserves such bad luck."

Kari spent the night as Hild's guest, and he slept long and deep. In the morning, he thanked her for her advice and rode away.

4 The Broken Man

As Kari rode back over the High Moor, he saw a dale that stretched away to the south, so he went down into its woods and searched them until he found a rowan tree. From its branches he cut the arrows that Hild had told him to make, and when they were ready he went on his way.

He spent the night in Westerdale, where he told his parents all he had learnt. In the morning he asked his father for the loan of his best hunting bow.

"I only wish," said Olaf, "that I could lend you my luck as well. You will be needing more of it than most men get in a lifetime."

Kari rode on and came to Colman's Dale. The

farmstead was eerily quiet. When he walked in
he saw Colman slumped in his chair and Grim
sitting by the fire shelling some withered
yellow peas.

"Where is Ellen?" he asked.

"Sick in her sleeping-chamber," replied
Grim.

Kari found her lying on a bed of crushed
bracken. The colour had drained from her skin
and her arms lay limp on the coverlet.

"What is the matter?" he asked.

"The wasting sickness has hold of me," she
whispered, in a voice that was less than an
echo of its former music. "It had to come.
There is no goodness in anything we eat or
drink here. This is the sickness that took my
mother, and now it is taking me."

"You must fight it," he pleaded. "I know a

way to break the spell. By sunrise the world will be well again."

Ellen smiled and lifted a pale hand to brush his cheek with her fingertips. "Poor Kari," she whispered, "I do love you and all your rash promises."

Kari held her hand until she fell asleep, then tore himself away from her and went back into the hall. The sight of Colman sitting staring at his feet made him want to scream.

"Shame on you for not taking Ellen away from here," he said reproachfully.

Colman looked at him with empty eyes. "She should never have been born," he replied.

Kari wanted to shake him until the teeth rattled in his head. "How can you say that about a daughter who will die rather than leave you?" he asked. "You must have the heart of a rabbit."

Colman gave a dry cackle. "That is my curse, Norseman. I have no heart left in me."

"Why?" asked Kari. "Tell me."

Colman slumped deeper into his chair, but a flicker of life came into his eyes. "Many years

34

ago in Ireland my heart was full of Catha, the daughter of the king of Connaught. I was a man of no fame and had no hope of marrying her, but we loved each other, and there was glory

in that. Then it came to the ears of the king, and I had to flee from Ireland to save my own life. And that is how I left my heart behind.''

"Still," said Kari, "I do not see the curse in that.''

"I gave Catha a vow," replied Colman, "that as long as I lived I would hold no other woman in my arms. But exile is long, and loneliness is deep, and glory can soon be forgotten, and when I came here I met Ellen's mother and made her my wife. Then it began. I searched

myself from head to heart but could find no
love to give her, and Ellen was born without
love. That is my curse, that I have no love, and
it has blighted me and mine ever since.''

The flicker went out of Colman's eyes and he
raised his drinking horn to his lips. Night was
falling.

"Perhaps my father is right,'' said Kari, "and
the breaking of another man's curse is way
beyond my luck, but I still intend to try what I
came here to try. Some good may come of it,
and anything is better than waiting for Ellen
to die.''

He took his bow and the arrows of rowan
and went out into the darkness to wait for the
Shape-Changer. The dale sank into a silence
broken only by the shuffling of the cattle in the
garth. Kari slipped into a dream in which he and

Ellen were living on a farm of their own, and the dream was so strong that it lulled him to sleep.

When he awoke, Ellen was standing above him, smiling in the moonlight. In her hands she held an elmwood bowl.

"All is well," she said. "I feel stronger now that you are here, and I have come for a drink of milk while it is safe in your protection."

He wanted to weep with happiness at the sight of her tossing back her hair as she knelt down to milk one of the cows. She drank a bowlful of milk in a single gulp and laughed.

"I feel so thirsty," she said, "and so full of life."

Kari laughed with her, and feasted his eyes on her as she went round the herd, milking the cows dry and drinking as she milked. Then a chill of doubt seized him and he walked quickly into the farmhouse. Another Ellen was lying in her bed of crushed bracken, and her breaths were weak and far between.

He ran outside. The shape of Ellen had milked the last cow dry and was licking her lips, and

Kari had never seen anyone so beautiful as the girl who came skipping towards him in the moonlight. His fingers trembled as he fitted an arrow to his bow.

"What are you doing?" asked the girl in horror.

He took aim at her ankle.

"Kari, no!" she cried. "It is me, Ellen."

"You are not Ellen," he said. "You are the Shape-Changer."

"No," she wailed. "This is the spell at work.

The spell has poisoned your mind.''

Kari drew back the bowstring and levelled his gaze down the arrow-shaft.

"Look at me!" she wailed.

He looked up into her eyes in the same moment that he loosed the arrow. It flew harmlessly past her and splashed into the stream.

"Fool," said the girl in a voice which was colder and darker than Ellen's had ever been. Then the shape changed and Kari found himself looking at the black wolf with the glowing yellow eyes. It bared its fangs, snarled, and bounded away into the trees.

5 Kari's Run

Kari seized his two remaining arrows and
sprinted through the wood, but when he came
out onto the moor the wolf was nowhere to be
seen.

He walked along the brow of the dale.
Everything was silent. The moor stretched away
from him, grey and silver in the moonlight.
Never had it looked so empty.

He turned his back on it and stared down at
the wood below him. The trees cast black pools
of shadow which twisted as though they were
alive. As he listened he heard the sound of
something scuffling in the undergrowth.

"No," he muttered, "I'm not coming in there
after you. Up here I stand between you and

your lair, and sooner or later you'll have to try and get past me."

He settled down to wait and had not been there long when he saw his father walking up out of the dale towards him.

"Help me, son," called Olaf. "A strange spell has fallen on Westerdale and your mother and brothers are sick. I need you to come home with me now."

"I have a feeling," said Kari, "that if I went home now I would find my father asleep in his bed."

He fitted a second arrow to his bow and aimed it at the shape of Olaf, which changed at once into a hare and streaked past him out onto the open moor.

Kari chased after it as fast as he could, but however hard he ran the hare ran faster, and

the gap between them began to widen. As soon as they reached a level stretch of moor where he could keep the hare in sight, Kari dropped to his knees and fired off his second arrow. It passed within a finger's breadth of the hare's hindlegs and disappeared into a peat bog.

"This has gone on long enough," said the cold, dark voice, "and it is time to make an end of it."

The hare changed shape and became a huge white mare with red eyes and breath steaming from red nostrils. She reared up on her

hindlegs and kicked at the sky with ironshod
hooves, then lowered her head and came
charging across the moor straight at Kari. His
mind filled with a sound of drumming hooves
which grew so deafening that he could hardly
think.

"Ellen," he whispered, "guide my hand
now." At the last moment he fired his third
arrow and flung himself sideways into the
heather.

The mare screamed with a human voice and
reared up, flailing at the air with her hooves.
Straight through one of them was the arrow of
rowan wood.

"A clever blow that," she said, "but I can
still outrun the wind."

The mare turned and galloped away over the
moor, so fast that great clods of peat were sent

flying by her hooves. Kari staggered to his feet just in time to watch her disappear over the skyline.

"Ellen," he whispered, "now you must guide my sight."

He set off in pursuit and ran crouching with his eyes on the ground. He had learnt as a small boy to read the tracks made by sheep over a moor of heather, and the marks of the ironshod hooves were easy enough to follow.

They led him up hill and down dale until two thirds of the night was past and still they stretched ahead of him over endless moor. Soon he could run no longer and slowed to a walk. He walked until his ribs ached and his tongue hung out and his legs lost all feeling. Twice he fell flat on his face in the heather and the moor seemed to spin round and round him like a whirlpool.

The dark night sky was paling to grey when he came to the edge of the furthest moor and found himself looking down on the green vastness of the northern plains.

The tracks of the mare veered away along the brow towards a great pointed hill which stood out from the edge of the moor. Kari took one look at its steep sides and groaned aloud. Gasping for every breath, he followed the hoofmarks up the hill, clutching at the bracken to steady himself as his feet slid on the slippery grass.

In the last of the moonlight he arrived at the foot of the crag of rust-coloured rock which was the summit of the hill. There, lying in the mouth of a cave, was the white mare.

Kari lunged forward and twisted his hands into the horse's mane.

"You will never escape me now," he said.

"Nor have I the strength to," said the mare, in a voice which seemed almost to be laughing at him. "A good chase that, and you had better tell me what it is you want from me."

"First of all, the answer to a question," he said. "Is it you who laid the spell of wasting on Colman's Dale?"

"It is," replied the mare, "but what is that to you?"

"The answer to your own question," said Kari. "It is the lifting of the spell I want from you."

The mare laughed. "Then you can wait and wait until ice covers the world, but the curse will not be lifted."

"Yes it will," said Kari. "I will lift it at sunrise when I see you in your true shape and gain power over you."

"Small power that," said the mare, "for it will only last as long as the sunlight, and at moonrise you will lose your hold on me and I will be free to work my spell again. Fool are you to think you can overcome my magic. To

48

save Colman you would need to stand guard
over his farmstead every night for the rest of
your life, and there are shapes I can take that
can never be pierced by arrows of rowan."

Kari mustered his wits for one last bluff.

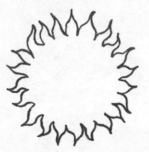

"But I will have the power of the sunlight,"
he said threateningly.

"And what is that?" asked the mare. "The
power to change my shape and to command my
movement, but no more. The power to break

the spell is mine alone, and you will never command it."

"It will be enough," he cried. "I will command you to ride over the top of this crag, and the spell will die with you."

"Poor victory that," said the mare, "for so will Ellen."

Kari closed his eyes and laid his face down in the cold dew of the grass. He had run out of words and run out of luck. He was empty of

everything except a longing for sleep and a desire for peace.

"Ellen . . ." he whispered.

It was then that the first ray of dawn touched the slopes of the hill.

6 Magic at Sunrise

As soon as the sunlight splashed onto the mare, her shape began to shimmer and shift, and Kari found that his fingers were no longer twisted into a horse's mane but wound into the hair of a beautiful woman. She wore a cloak of green over a dress of crimson, and her eyes and hair were the red-gold of beech leaves in autumn. He stood back and gasped.

"Now you see the truth of me," she said, "though it will not tell you much."

"It tells me everything, for you can only be Catha, the daughter of the king of Connaught."

"That I am," she replied, "and much sorrow has it brought me."

"Less than it has brought Colman," said Kari.

"He betrayed me," cried Catha. "I followed him across the sea, but long I was in coming, and when I found him I saw he had taken another woman to his hearth. The love turned to hate in my heart, and for that I cursed him."

She began to weep, and Kari filled with pity. He took hold of her ankle and pulled out the arrow of rowan, then cleaned the wound with dew-soaked grass.

"I wish I had not had to hurt you," he said.

As he spoke the wound disappeared and her ankle was whole again.

"How did that happen?" he asked.

"Through the power of your magic," said Catha.

"My magic?" he repeated, scratching his head. "There is nothing magic about me."

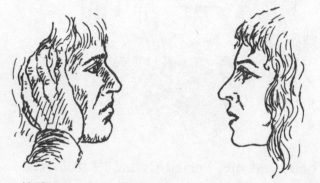

"There is the magic of your love for Ellen," she replied. "For magic can only be born out of the two strongest feelings, and they are love and hate. The magic of love has the power to do good, and the magic of hate has the power to do bad. It is the magic of love which gave you the strength to hunt me down."

"Then perhaps I have the power to break the spell?" said Kari.

"Perhaps," agreed Catha, "but spells made with hate are the hardest to break, and you have only the length of this sunlight."

"Then we will not sit here talking. I command you to change back into the white mare."

Catha vanished and the white mare appeared. Kari sprang onto her back.

"Now I command you to carry me to Colman's Dale."

The white mare tossed her head and cantered obediently down the slopes of the hill. Soon she was galloping across the top of

the moors, and Kari rode with the sun in his
eyes and a wind blowing in his face that left
the taste of sea salt on his lips. The sun was
still climbing the sky when they came to the
brow of the moor and looked down into
Colman's Dale. Kari jumped to the ground and
patted the mare's neck.

"And now," he said, "change into an eight-
week-old kitten."

The horse vanished and Kari saw a small
black kitten blinking up at him from amongst

a clump of heather. He picked it up and stroked
it and tucked it between his shirt and his tunic.

"Keep still and hidden," he said, "and listen
well to everything you hear."

He walked down into the farmhouse and
found Colman and Grim sitting exactly where
he had left them the night before.

"How goes it with Ellen?" he asked.

"She is fading while we sit here," said
Colman. He looked at Kari with eyes that were
emptier than ever. "And how goes it with you?
Have you come to tell me you can break the
spell?"

"I have," said Kari, "and I will if you can
answer me three questions. The first of them
is this – What is the cause of this curse you feel
lying on you?"

57

"Not difficult that," replied Colman. "I have been cursed since the day I broke my vow to Catha of Connaught."

"And who is the woman you have loved most in your life?"

"Not difficult that," replied Colman. "Catha of Connaught."

"And when was the last time you tasted happiness?"

"Not difficult that. It was the day before I parted with Catha of Connaught."

As Colman finished speaking Kari felt a dampness against his chest. The kitten was crying, and its tears had soaked through his

58

shirt. He lifted it out of his tunic and placed it on the floor.

"It seems to me," he told it, "that you will be loved in your true shape."

The kitten vanished and Catha appeared in all her beauty. Colman's eyes gaped open and he shook in every limb of his body, then he dropped to his knees and threw his arms around her waist.

"Forgive me," he said. "Forgive me for trying to forget you."

Catha's tears ran faster and she cradled his head in her hands. "It is you who must forgive me," she said. "Forgive me for forgetting my

love for you and for using my power to keep you from happiness." She turned to Kari. "The spell is broken," she said. "You have released us all from the magic of hate."

"Then I have one last command," he said, "to turn the power back into the magic of love. Change Ellen so she is well again, change Grim's leg so he is no longer lame, and change

your own shape and Colman's so you are once
again the way you were on the day you first
met.''

All this happened at once. Catha and Colman
laughed and clung to each other, Grim began
to leap up and down, and Ellen walked out of
the sleeping-chamber with pink in her cheeks
and a spring in her step.

Ellen took one look at her father laughing with joy, then she ran outside and sang the Three Songs of Rejoicing. At the first song the flowers that should have blossomed in spring came out all over the dale. At the second song the cows of the dairy herd each gave birth to a calf. At the third song the barley and the wheat harvests came up together. As she

finished, she saw Kari standing watching her
from the doorway.

"I have a feeling," she said to him, "that my
father will not be needing me by his hearth for
much longer."

"I know someone who will," he said quickly.

It was not long after that that Kari and Ellen were married and built their own farmstead up at Westerdale Head. They were more than happy, and everyone who knew them called them the Luck Bringers. Over the years they had five children, and there are many stories worth telling about them, but this is the end of the story of the Shape-Changer of Colman's Dale.

Julian Atterton lives in Castleton, North Yorkshire and from the room where he works at the top of his house, he has a wonderful view up the valley and over the moors. He has written several historical novels and two Storybooks centred on tales of Robin Hood.

When he is not writing and researching, he likes to indulge in his favourite hobby, rock-climbing, which he does primarily in the north of England and France; he has also climbed in the Atlas Mountains.

Here are some more **WALKER STORYBOOK** titles for you to enjoy

STAPLES FOR AMOS

by Alison Morgan

(black and white illustrations
by Charles Front)

When Mum forgets to
buy staples for Amos
to mend the fence of the
bullock field, Daley acts quickly to try
and save her from the
anger of the old farm
worker. But his action
leads him into danger...

"A story of courage and determination...
A simple, imaginative and rather
moving tale."
British Book News

A WALKER STORYBOOK

We Three Kings From
PEPPER STREET PRIME

by Joan Smith

(black and white illustrations by
Nicole Goodwin)

Pepper Street Primary's
Christmas concert is
never a dull affair –
chaotic, yes, but dull,
no. This year, with the
lively Em playing the Virgin
Mary and her football-mad younger
brother in the supportng
cast, the production looks
like being even
more colourful
and chaotic than
usual!

A WALKER STORYBOOK

EARTHQUAKE

by Ruskin Bond

(black and white illustrations by
Valerie Littlewood)

"What do you do when there's
an earthquake?" asks Rakesh.
Everyone in the Burman
household has their own
ideas, but when the tremors
begin and everything starts to shake and
quake, to crack and
crumble, they are
taken by surprise...

A WALKER STORYBOOK

ROBIN HOOD

and the
MILLER'S SON

by Julian Atterton

(black and white illustrations by
John Dillow)

When Much the Miller's son is
seized by the cruel Sir
Guy of Gisburn,
Robin Hood is
determined to
save him. To do
so, he enlists the
help of Marian, her father, Sir Gilbert,
and Will Scarlet. But when
the day of his daring rescue
comes, Robin's greatest ally
is a giant shepherd called
John...

A WALKER STORYBOOK

ROBIN HOOD
and *LITTLE JOHN*

by Julian Atterton

(black and white illustrations by
John Dillow)

One day, when walking
in the forest, Robin
Hood encounters a
huge stranger – and
ends up in the river!
The man is, of course,
Little John and he and Robin
soon become the best of
friends. But Little John
brings with him a
problem – a dangerous
challenge for Robin
and his men...

A WALKER STORYBOOK

Walker Books also publishes a range of entertaining novels by top authors. The stories cover a variety of subjects and situations – historical, adventure, suspense, horror, sci-fi, comedy and lots more. You'll find more information on some of these novels over the page.

VAMPIRE MASTER

Virginia Ironside

There's something very sinister about Burlap Hall's new biology master, Mr A. Culard. He hates light, loves bats and eats dead flies! Now the other teachers are starting to behave oddly too. The question is: will young Tom and his friends, Susan and Miles, manage to get their teeth into the problem before it gets its teeth into them?

"A very funny novel which keeps up a steady pace of entertainment and suspense."
The Bookseller

"Entertaining. . . Hilarious moments."
Junior Bookshelf

THE HORN OF MORTAL DANGER

Lawrence Leonard

When Jen and her brother Widgie stumble across a secret underground world, they find themselves in the middle of a war between two rival factions, the Railwaymen and Canal Folk. It is the start of a thrilling and dangerous adventure.

"A fantasy whose words are forcefully visual, whose concept is original and compelling."
Growing Point

"A lively, original and exciting adventure story."
The Times Literary Supplement

ANANCY-SPIDERMAN

James Berry

Anancy, the hero of these twenty lively and intriguing Afro-Caribbean folk tales, is both man and spider. Seemingly defenceless, he is an artful rogue who uses his cunning to out-wit his opponents – the mighty Bro Tiger in particular. But these are just two in a colour-ful cast of characters which includes Bro Dog, Bro Monkey, Old Higue Dry-Skull, Swing-Swing Janey and many, many more.

"James Berry retells these vivid stories . . . in a soft, mellifluous voice that captures the magic and trickery of the spider hero."
Julia Eccleshare, Children's Books of the Year